THE POEMS' OF JOHN WM. GILES

John Wm. Giles

The Poems' Of John Wm. Giles

Author: John Wm. Giles

Copyright © John Wm. Giles (2023)

The right of John Wm. Giles to be identified as author of this work has been asserted by the author in accordance with section 77 and 78 of the Copyright, Designs and Patents Act 1988.

First Published in 2023

ISBN 978-1-83538-017-8 (Paperback)
978-1-83538-018-5 (E-book)

Cover Illustration 'GILES' by Peter Crow 1967

Cover Design and Book Layout by:
    White Magic Studios
    www.whitemagicstudios.co.uk

Published by:
    Maple Publishers
    Fairbourne Drive, Atterbury,
    Milton Keynes,
    MK10 9RG, UK
    www.maplepublishers.com

A CIP catalogue record for this title is available from the British Library.

All rights reserved. No part of this book may be reproduced or translated by any form or by any means, electronic or mechanical, including photocopying, recording or by any information storage and retrieval system without written permission from the author.

The views expressed in this work are solely those of the author and do not necessarily reflect the views of the publisher, and the publisher hereby disclaims any responsibility for them.

CONTENTS

The Parousia Variations Poems

1. Summer, Folkestone, Poetry, me 8
2. Dawn Image 9
3. A White Bird Wing Flutters 10
4. Cubic Christ 11
5. The Argument 12
6. Meadow Image 13
7. The Copulation of Cancer 14
8. Decayed Stamen 16
9. The Cleansing Masonry 17
10. Perhaps By Chance 18
11. Rust Stains 19
12. The Summer Girl 20
13. He Had So Much Love That It Died 22
14. Eating With Charcoal Girl 26
15. Fight 28
16. The Nine Colours 29
17. Pub Reflections 31
18. Isadora 32
19. Kamala 33
20. Riding Jerusalem 34

21. Punter...35

22. Sunny Friday 36

23. Corroded Flesh Loving.....................................38

24. Night Image 40

25. The Hearth Imp...41

26. Vagitus...42

27. Indictment...43

28. Shuttered Grey Eyes..44

29. Ungeziefer...45

30. Renovating Glass..46

31. Again And Again...47

32. Ever Ending...48

33. Dark Prism..50

34. Kerouac's Gerard..51

35. Glass Ear 52

36. The Inconvenience...53

37. Apheliotropic..54

38. Just a Holding...55

39. Parousia..56

40. An Epilogue-The Nether World......................58

CONTENTS

Swansongs In Nightshade

1. Worms Within 60
2. Broken Flame...62
3. Haiku 64
4. Handel Night And Morn (Remembrance Sunday) 65
5. Firing An Empty_gun 67
6. My Sweet Zheng Shu 69
7. The Photograph 70
8. Old Bitch..72
9. Lace 73
10. Emma 75
11. Bone Ash 76
12. The Troubles 78
13. Richard 79
14. Lust...80
15. Mushrooms..81
16. Argo..82
17. Camera Obscura..83
18. Rioja Lips 85
19. Sabastina..86

20. Kyrie..87

21. Little Sticks...88

22. Bus Stop..89

23. Decay 90

24. Lone Utterances..91

25. Hunger A Day...92

26. For I Am The Vine Dresser 93

27. Drinking Song...95

28. Gaia Girl..97

29. Broken Morning..98

30. Anastasia 1918... 100

31. Full Gifted Was His Sight............................... 102

32. Suicide... 104

33. Upon The Plains of Absalom 105

34. "Sheila 1966".. 107

35. Rain 109

36. Strange Birds.. 111

37. For Marion.. 113

38. Sunday, Puccini As Usual.............................. 114

39. Soft Skinning Girls 115

The Parousia Variations Poems

For
'Shirley'

Summer, Folkestone, Poetry, me

'Her voice
        Went along
                The promenade quietly.'

Dawn Image

A patch of black earth,
The young yellow crocus bud,
Uplifting itself
To the cold dawning light
In an instant,
A burst of life,
A startled blackbird in flight.

John Wm. Giles

A White Bird Wing Flutters

The pin cushion fell
Lightly to the floor,
Followed the slender white hand
To retrieve its lost possession,
A white fluttering bird wing
In a slow gentle movement of sewing,
The scarlet shawl
Embroidered with gold thread,
Wavering the white bird hand
Moves in its flight,
Along its seam
With golden stream trailing,
The fluttered wing
Silent in its flight,
Slows to rest,
Sleep the scarlet shawl, finished.

Cubic Christ

How crisp is remembrance,
The cubic Christs head
Rest on soft sponges,
Sour the lips with vinegar,
Muttering earth chains
With the scissors of love,
He cut the bonding chords
From the joints of sin,
Foundations crumbled
Under the flow of his blood.
Eye lids cut perceiving light
Upon the earthly grave.
Jesus to people gave
Coloured weeping stones
Bedlam of his speech.

The Argument

Drawing away the scarf
From her stabbing lips,
She spoke with witless voice
Of bittering words.

I stretched forth the cigarette
Letting the ash fall,
Before the words broke its motion
Over stale pools,
Her savaging my brain
Soaking up the wine.

The Parousia Variations Poems

Meadow Image

In the meadow
The white calf
Butts the sapling.

The Copulation of Cancer

I hear
The fondles of death
And the utterance beyond.

Scared lines upon his book
The childs fingers arrested
The difficult spelling
The clarity of copperplate
Gave no meaning.

The sun had burnt his tears
A wrinkled sorrow upon his cheek
He will never forget the time
When the sea picked up his cry
And rent the sand
From beneath his feet
Drawing them scroll like
To her soul
Why had she left him so empty.

The child asked its mother
What the words meant,
Just a dream that her father
Once dreamt within shadows.

Close the book, for in are
Held the grapes of life
And the copulation of cancer.

Decayed Stamen

Early morning
I lounged in the old rocking- chair,
Blue dead flowers bending
To the studio window,
I see left standing in the cheap vase
Tired flowers match my own weariness,
The room still full of night
Yesterday was somehow too long.

Sitting quietly thoughtful
Surrounded by friends,
The talk that came across the table
Hit me softly, too softly.

Back to the room with its dead flowers

Reading poetry they were,
Turned to me with fingers to their mouths.
Would I be them or partly their abstractions,
All my windows are distorted
And I cannot see the truth.

The Cleansing Masonry

On the window-sill the slippery rain fell
In a torrent gush cleansing the masonry.
Within the walls hapless youths lie
Dreaming with the vigour brains of summer.
Unconnecting their youthful being
Within the rains torrent speech.

Holding fast their summer-dream
Against the winters coming screen,
Flickering from their eyes the films
Of knowledgeless child memory are screened.

Like rain the films evaporate
Into careless tears of youth.

Perhaps By Chance

Perhaps in chance we meet,
On a silver streamed boulevard.
Or upon entering a door left apart,
Perhaps by chance we close our hearts.
On this met long parting
Or close that door left long ajar,
Perhaps in chance I broke your heart.

Rust Stains

December solitude cold
Stood faced the sea
With its ever motion.
Song of salt grains
Veins in my hand showed
As I gripped the balustrade,
Voiced my cold faintness
To the continuous song of waves.
Apparently I was not alone
The bicycle man appeared below me.
Wheels making unoiled music of rust
Pausing, voiced a murderous oath.
Moved on playing his grinding song,
Gone, passed, I missed his rusting hate
Turned, and stepped back to quiet reality
Of a sea-side hotel in December.

John Wm. Giles

The Summer Girl

Grasshopper green pathways,
Those lost green paths, I walked,
And meet a summer girl
She's waiting on the sun-ships
Standing arrayed upon the flow.
Her gossamer hair tangled a teared eye
She let drop a golden sigh,
That drifted to my eye
And there we saw a sunflower die.
We move in echoes through the yarrow
Down to the sea and sand,
Reflect the amber to see the honey bee
With her colourful tambourine in hand,
She dances on the sand.
I stand shadowed
The cliff envelopes me,
As if I were a struck tree.
The day is turning scarlet
Is the sea permanently green
The chalk cliffs begin to scream,
Am I in a dream

Or do I hear Apes cry,
That on this day one of us will die
Cliff wall cracked, and fell,
And killed the summer girl.
In utter dismay and tears
I stood rooted heartbroken
And lost.

He Had So Much Love That It Died

When first we meet
Was it by eyes only
Or heart sweet one
The lemons in the bowl
Tearful fruit,
Her the lake stilled
Cooled by some breath
Your young breath my love
Purple purple wine of Italy.

A boat mine hired
Her many coloured sails gentle
Like some swan so light,
Her breast
Hardly touching the waters skin you.

I had just burnt my poems
When first we meet my love,
If meet we did?
Wine glass to lips staining
Were I not back home again from you.

The Parousia Variations Poems

Was it but a passing fancy
Image, beauty, lust.
Wanting a return to myself
My art burnt, forgotten.
Boy, boyhood in my own country
Corn poppy, love desire
Upon the lip open touch.

The sleeping form warmth closeness
A dog its hair, no yours
Body prone amongst the lemon grove
Succulent, bitter.
No never bitter, please
He had so much love
That he died not yet
Like morning after rain.

The quivering of the body
Ablaze with longing,
The heart fluctuant would burst
Like the sun at dawn for you.
Agony, fear, breaking the mind
With torrents of desire, for your touch.
All is futile, barren, hopeless
Never had loved so, much
That it died for you.

John Wm. Giles

The broken glass your broken words
Parting at spring tide,
Your youth consumed
Was it satisfied
Or choked with my love,
Solace day
When the minute even had length
Moment the hand leaving mine,
Rested amongst splintered crystal
Red with blood wine.
Your rudded cheeks,
Glinting tears turmoiled eyelash.
Lip never still,
The vicious words,
Unspeaking through stained lips
Your lips a flock of birds.
The sarcophagus heart finally violated
Your temple veil rendered,
Where was whiteness
Surely, but our parting skin,
The crimson patches remembered.

The Parousia Variations Poems

Your way was white, pure, undefiled,
My love was not, I our Bacchus,
Pan seeking the immersing glory
Of Dionysus form, fawn-skined one.
What broke us,
Your faith which lacked flesh-felts,
Liar!
He had no love that it died
The extinguishing.

Morning light upon our chaise-longue
Gleamed, lost.
Warming dawn of Italy.
The ridicule of yesterday,
Stuck like sweat to my hands,
Little one your hand vacant,
In this void morn.
I had so much love that it died
Consumpted in light.

Eating With Charcoal Girl

1

Hot meat and bones, stimulant to the bowl
The charcoal girl would help herself,
Picked the tenderest,
The tongue refused the sinews,
Her lips stung by peppered knowledge.

How long has she been here
Could I bring back the time,
There are recalled times
When she has laughed with me
Across many a 'chilled wine glass of poetry
And warm salmon flesh meals
In the restaurant of memory.

2

The breakfast-room overlooked the sea,
My charcoal girl had crumbled bread
Scented with tea and lemon
Eaten gently with the waters of my mouth.

The Parousia Variations Poems

Later in the morning she and I
Walk in fur coats down to the sea
When the breaking waves subdued the shingles
We hungered.

Fight

My Flamingo hand, bruised darkened
Likened itself to some Prometheus
Lost in flame and blood.

Razor of noise, splitting the mind,
Her little image shattered.

Lip moving into sorrow.

The Nine Colours

Days of summer and honey
And the youth of remembrance,
Sun-lapped the stream of shadows
Breaking through the branches
Before the silent way.
We step the day
Gently afraid of the growth
Of sun-fed vegetation
Before the coiled natures.
Dormant, cold,

Evening comes.

We sat with the love flow
In the corners of our mouths.
Flowers upon the beach
A rose is tangled, in the sand,
Thorns protrude to touch my hand.
Lap the waves
Into gentle figurines
Of past dreams,

Leaving ripples of mystic runes
Upon the shore.

And what now is left before
The chafed dawn.

Pub Reflections

The sanguine laugh
As if cutting from lips
Above the striking of a match.

The perspiration
Imprint of the hand
Upon the table-top.

Could it had been
Grained wood or sulphur fumes.

Isadora

Tragic Bugatti,
Fated shawl flowing,
Silver wheel spin,
Caught, pulled, strangled.

Kamala

Beneath the glass the tomatoes
Are ripening delicate as blood,
The books lie dormant upon the shelves
And the dust had settled on my fingertips.

The slope to the shingled beach
Gave warning of her coming,
The house had always been a sun-trap
The tomatoes ripened and I also

I had once seen a fox hunting a mole
He caught it, I recall the blood against
Its black fur,
Gave no warning of his coming.

And when I gripped the orange
The dust shifted
Unsettled to the floor.

Riding Jerusalem

Within the grains of marble
The fossilised chalk of night is hidden,
Jagged and white.

And was it sweet chilled raspberries
Losing their flavour amongst the ice,
Melting down the windows colours
An encroachment upon the room.

The last breakfast
Recall while upon his mule
Broken open to his scent.
And now the breakfast could they eat an oat
The seed of his meaning
Was it just an opium
Stifling their voices.

Somewhere the sword of tongues cut depth
openess
The boy his mouth hair,
Whiteness and the waters of his mouth
Upon the lips,
The dead coals of his winters fire ebbed.

Punter

Come now Jacob boy
Lift the hand,
The golden coin beneath
Will burn the skin,
The circle mark
The gamblers crease.

Sunny Friday

Down the walls the sun
Melts in white drifts,
Clinging to the peeling windows,
Hers filled with vacant sadness,
When friday fell in sunlight,
Upon her voice,
Speaking with words,
Chosen in haste,
The voice sounds,
Made hazey patterns,
I stood in shades,
Reading poetry from her walls,
What was her lover to me?
I had strayed to close
In her parabolic reflections,
Along sun-kissed cheeks.

The Parousia Variations Poems

I told her,
I had only dropped in
To see the poems he had left,
She screamed from her suicide leap
In the open sunlit window.

The sun glints,
The world has grown,
Very small.

Corroded Flesh Loving

Its time, and turning back
The face that once
Was my only picture.
The picture now faded,
With the air of losing you.
Corroded the hearts feelings,
Would that artist
Paint again your colour
Of loving me.

Now to see back the turning time
Your pale body laying
Next to nuptial linen.
Even that picture
Is faded in creased untidiness
Cold our sweat, and love lost.

The Parousia Variations Poems

The window that you left ajar
In your escape,
From our leaving tautness.
Memorable flesh, one skin
Merge with easiness of oil colour
In your picture of me
Back turn time,
My time, and yours, shortly.

Night Image

In the night,
The utterance of snails
Shaking the forest leaves,
Enters my window
Upon a breeze
Softly vibrating the pillow
Against my sleeping breath.

The Hearth Imp

Someone came,
Lingering upon the hearth.
Footprint in the ashes,
A'telling impatient waiting.
The someone came
Had help'd themselves
To tea and bible.
Silken cord moved
Displaced amongst Psalms.
Copper kettle half empty
Perhaps a journeyman,
Seeking shelter from the storm.

Vagitus

The renovating glass
He held before me, fused.
The talking soul his whisper
Throat vocalic spitting filth.
Soiled broke the vein
The white arm.
Pours forth her crimson water
Before him laughter.
My love,
Is it now our parting wanes
A crimson flow
The white body throbs
The heat of my birth
Left me silently.

Indictment

With a draft of words and wine
I vomited in ignorance.
Their apathy drew the meanings together
But within I felt the dawning spite,
Where was my gentle soul, darkened, shielded,
Within the grape, her yielding redness,
Stifling growth and spirit.
But I felt a sweetness
At morning-tide

And I took the sand away
From under my finger-nails.

I remember that nails
Should recollect a thought
But I am insufficient.

Shuttered Grey Eyes

The house I knew long ago
Had shuttered grey-eyes.
Seniled and decayed from its portal
The growth of broccoli spears out front
Tinged her solemn hues.
As a lad I thought the succulent vegetables
Devoured by old grey-eyes.
It was never picked,
Merely over-ripened, faded.
One summer old grey-eyes burnt down,
Her heat burnt my hand,
Her roasted broccoli consumed my youth.

And the house I knew once long ago
Had shuttered grey-eyes.

Ungeziefer

Eva 'Eva'...as I was just saying
He didn't come up the third time!
We don't think he minded much,
He wouldn't have liked it
Where we were about to go.
...Crack of almonding glass!..
Bitch! that's why they call us
Stigmating Cains,
For all is night in us.
...Crack!..............
Muffled discharge echoes forever,
Berlin's suiciding bunker
Recoiling pierced souls.

Renovating Glass

Mirror distorting.

The academy uppermost in his mind,
Where only bistre was used,
Artless colour,
The spine of the moon shaken.
Mimicking lips taken innocence by words
The child burnt black in the time-sun
Anguish the back bent and broken,
Final utterance.

I have renovating glass.

Again And Again

Mother with child
Dead in the street.
War began again today,
Is it no one
Gives a damn?
Or is it me.
Would that God
Would hate his creation.
Crumple it up
Like a paper ball
And toss it to his
Everlasting flames.
If he`s not sick of it
I am.

Ever Ending

From early evenings spring balcony
The dull sun rested herself upon me,
Bringing that wind to blow through
Like Cassius's despairing sword,
I waiting upon my muse
Where is now my bold woman?
She has left me
To toy with other lovers,
In my soul.

These maudling children
Within grumbling,
Snatching the crumbs
From sister frustrations table,
Over-spilling the wine
Of my hard wrought poetry.

I but left seeking
My own perdition,
Hark!
Dido's plaintive 'remember me'
In my heart.

Echo sorrowing echo.

Tears.

Cheek turning to the open door
Pain ever ending,
Ever ending.

Ending ever.

Dark Prism

What sea? What boat this?
Ego rising, Leviathans tail
Like some dark angel.
Above lifes languishing mediocrity
Fills with lust, soon burnt,
Spent the world.
That unfair master
A serfdom of self-deceptions, loneliness
Leaving only dark corners of solituding
Where serpent futility sits.
Boa-ing hope. swallowing faith.
Vomit stifling its child screams,
Drips his epitaph.
'Man thy glory,
But a grizzled gibbet of wants'.

Asmondeus, put the book down, and sighed.

Kerouac's Gerard

All the spite in the world
Cannot stop these tears,
For that Christ child
Pulled by carted lambs.

Glass Ear

Poet of glass ear
Splinted to Gods glare
Poetical stare.
Could he speak beauty
From within his cold tear
Of loves unequivalent.
And could I love
The pity of the poets purity,
Hear words in bled hearts meaning,
Only to witness gods form burst,
In the creating.

The Inconvenience

In this dark place,
Where the little children sit
And talk to me of things,
That could have been.
These aborted murders, laugh and play,
Singing joy into my face.
Asking me what its like to be a father-mother,
Living in the light and caring for one another.
I can only weep too tell,
That they do not live, in light or love.
But take and use, leaving only their wastings,
Even these, they gave you no chance to,
You would have been a surfeiting.
But you can ask them themselves,
For they are coming to join us, one day,
On Judgment day.

Apheliotropic

The distance moves the friends apart,
Till nearly forgotten, remember.
An egg hidden in the warm wheat sheaf
Generating humid waves upon the birds cells.
Who had put the egg there knew little
That it would not break open and live.
The gatherers boot crushed
Crystal ooze and blood speck.
Shattered by pressure
Flecked shell spreading upon jelly
From under calf leather.
Staining, remember, weep,
Natural and naked.

Just a Holding

I want someone to take me,
In a holding closeness.
Be held so tightly in their scent,
Hear the beat of a heart against my skin.
Let me not fall into my own despair.

Just hold me with a kindness and nothing more.
Let not my own darkness,
Tear me from your muzzling warmth,
That dark me, he will I know
Drag and rip me back into myself.

God save me from what I have become.
Give me your mercy and in so doing
Let love of another,
Shield me from my afflicting death.

Parousia

While shifting my timeless sands
Upon all the least of my broken promises.
I came up against that one
Which is ever unbreakable.
Life in all its agonizing length,
That well rooted thing, gripping so tightly
Holding pain ever in the heart and mind,
Always hurting in the daylight,
Waiting, realizing eternal rest.
From O, so real flesh and blood reality
That is a thing known.
Insisting in its own knowledge
All joy and sorrow moments inserted.
To give the Gnosis of self-hope
That God does and will so love us
In our diverse endings.
For are we not his timeless sands
Upon ethereal shores
Ever lapped by our unbelief,
In ourselves and him.

The Parousia Variations Poems

But how long can I hold
A belief that his little Holy son
Jesus, playing on those eternal shores
With bucket and spade, lovingly
Making sand-castles of our souls.

The omniscient wind fluttering,
Our little paper flags of redemption
Amongst sun bleached shells.

An Epilogue-The Nether World

And I stood with my
Broken ashtray in my hand

In the end there was nothing.

Swansongs In Nightshade

For
'All Those Who Love Me'

John Wm. Giles

Worms Within

My mind is lurking
On the underside of the table,
Those around me only see the surface
Why will they not lie on their backs.
The natural underside of us all
Is so much more inviting,
For is this not where the beetle attacks first,
We only recognize this worm-beetle
When they burst through our shinny surface
Making a mockery or profundity
In the minds of those who knew us not.
Do we so long for our sheen only
Forever trying to hide the eruptions
Or do we really relish on tender-hooks
The bursting forth of our darkness and light,
To end up scratched or french -polished
Both a problem, how to hide the scratches
Or keep the mirrored surface pure....
, An erupting beetle has moved my thoughts,
Elemental force of rain tapping my windows
Was it not a avian altercation on sill,

Swansongs In Nightshade

Sparrow chased away by starling
Mottled beaked scavenger
Harsh malevolent caller, breaking my flow,
Is it eagerness for life that sent you thus
Encroaching upon my white sheet and black words,
You have now inserted yourself
With the gable, overhung with water, falling,
Later in the evening those stagnant waters
Fill up gaps to drip inside my souls necessity

'Twere but all this a swan
And I Lohengrin

"Tis but me worm eaten.

Broken Flame

Never listen
Friends poison
Breeds loss
Loss, old friend of mine
Breeds half-breeds
Infecting my tribe
So well, make me a smallpox blanket
Choked buffalo, blood snorted
Carcass rotting, children rotting

That was then
Back to myself
Cadaver
Self dissect
Open all the scores
Hoping nothing more
A lick on slit lip
Too many words

Holding compass fingers
Lobster thumb and finger
To snuff flame

You black stalk
I a last un-catchable smoke.

Haiku

Hoar-frosted bramble
Hush, quietly
Hare staring at the moon.

Handel Night And Morn (Remembrance Sunday)

Sitting separated from me
Rooms distance, spoke a universe
I sucking a black hole
They would now go to see where that bus
Would take her, just after five each morn,
Too that not quite lost life
Sorrowing their not forsaken children
In tears and acquainted in grief

Knowingly, I stepped out

Petra sunk into my head
After shaking your hand,
Burgundy blazer, fits this working man
Like a glove, have we met in another life,
Amongst petra's decaying sheer faces
A remembrance before our drinks set in,
Made places in my days, when was only given
To those sweet souls, who would or would not
Asked unto me, i freely gave comrades all
Spake that our day would come

John Wm. Giles

Drifted lashed to the raft, masefield salting
My ears, scuttled in the night, lighthouse in sight
Who's air drowned like a woman,
Me 'thought I saw something alight, 'twas nothing
But her scent made odious in my sight,
Back to my grandchild in light

She wakeful for her mother
Up and down within parted hours,
Back to bed my sweet one with simba and ladybird
Let softly night smother you lest tears bring
You and me crying strauss's last four songs
Till dawn, comrade to bed, only leaving me
I a lacquered brush, softly moved over, so softly
Moved over what was

From this now sorry window
The sea-gulls line roofs
Gizzards full of vomit,
But another morning, beholden your god,
Poet, jesu my saviour, held and lend me to sherry

The child's up
Fields of light,

Firing An Empty_gun

Erik satie 2.30 morning
Yellowing end
Of hand-made cigarette
No poetry in me
This my life
Drew boldly the last draw
I worthless poet
But who am I to say

Satie plays
I over tired with drink
3 Days now
As usual
Ever waiting my muse
Long dead I think
Summered my roses

What is all this
Fuck it
Back to my vodka
Brooding a quick dawn
Mammoth moved
Starling strut

John Wm. Giles

An after-thought
The children you give
All your love to
Don't even want to know
No understanding
This old mammoth
Bleeding the dead starlings

It's now gone 3.30
I've stopped the music
But not the inner pain

Lugt, schwestern
Die weckerin lacht in den grand
Wagner slung into my face
Turned to peter paul and mary
All my trials lord will soon be over
Thank god
Thank fuck

Cursing my life
In my last vodka
And now to sleep
Liar

Wings flapping
My face.

My Sweet Zheng Shu

Trilling flutes
Delicacy her voice

My back to her
Clipped mulberry leaves
Razor toning
For hungry wormy silks
Insatiable
Renders me work for life
But not for her
Age will take her songs away
My fading linnet companion

What am I to do
Looking down before dawn
Upon her sleeping form
She will lark my morning
Above the worms calling

My sweet zheng shu
Softer than the chains
That bind me to emperor cloth.

The Photograph

Sitting sad faced,
Clutching wooden train.
Was the colour hand tinted
Matt hues inside open eyes,
A world of truth
Not yet given and closed
On this my childhood.
In years passing through corn and poppy,
Holding water bottle
And well cut bread and butter,
Secure in leather satchel.
Beneath pylons isolate, fed I myself.
Distant view of Essex lost village,
Who's name forgotten,
To see stocks and lockup,
So distant in me now.
Sorely used my memory,
But screaming at her innocence
Those things which when were young,
Did stand so loose upon me.

My life now
A book of mounted negatives.

Yes, comrade
I stood with the oiled Eskimo,
Shutting out the photograph
Of the dreaming child.

Old Bitch

To have a poet in residence
Brings a pub a certain ambiance

Sitting next to the aged bird
Vulture in affluence
Made rich, die rich
You august bitch
Who never bought me a drink
Unacceptable though this is
(I call this a damn disgrace,
Not to buy a poet a libation)
Still, I will speak kindly at your death
Rat poison to you, you, you old bitch
We're drink it together,
In the flames of gabriel.

Lace

The lace
The lace
Are we working
Curtains, softening body garment
Or more softer still a greening wing

The lace
Conjurer fingers aged now,
But what have these fingers
Seen wars and loss
I held them momentary
Released, bobbins crossed
Her carrying a greater cross, than I
Left taking the ordered package

Knuckled mouth I moved
Opened the gates of greening
Lace wings
Biting my emotions

Yellow moon hung
Soaking indigo
Frosting lamp-posts
Moved I, ever so slowly
Into the waters of babylon

I wings laced
Emotions biting, bittering.

Emma

The hunchback and the poet
(After my frequenter of many beer-halls)

Shadow boxed the avenue
Stupefied spoon rendezvous
Me a mere renegade
Like shelley's ozymandias
Within a vastness penetrating no light
I also stood alone
Will they tremble words
Made known, if this were so easy
I'd be emma pulling her sweat-shirt back
To scratch long and lovingly
The top of her breast
Blue veins suffused pinking crimson
Like unto a lovers bite

Rest awhile my fleeting cheek
Soft pressed with that beating heart.

Bone Ash

Saw creeping bones
Creeping living bones
Living in my bones
Attached from air
Formed on their own accord
Sunk into my leg
Another bad day
Night if you will
Bones are bones
I true unto myself
You read unknowing
My sweet ones
Accurser spat
Back chewing bastard
Phoned later
Ended up with so much ash
Grey fingers
Accursing
All the haunting bridges

Swansongs In Nightshade

In semi-shadows
A fisher bird
Wings enfolding
Sighs

The Troubles

The day before they wept
Acrimony came scoring
Who will trouble
Cuchulain's seed
Sitting in the
Dead fire places

Richard

Summer evening in the park
Richard the third
Grass overlaying, stoney to arse
Players well tried
Incorporating bards words
Pantomime, children up close
Richard took the boos and heckles
Till he in fear forward came
Children silenced in the soft rain
To hear deeds dark untold
Little-ones, now's your turn
With ghostly princes
Hands sworded
Parrying the garden
Their cheers rung
Made grass bloody
On bosworth's field.

Lust

Wishing a surfeit
Of a woman's body
With devouring mouths
That raw energy
That only she has
I don't care if
I spent to quick
Flesh and fluids
Too while me hours
Till strength
Returns her smile
To pump and mash
Her sweet beguile

My pleasure to comb
Her hair with my honey,

Mushrooms

Child in the rain
Holding mushrooms

I soft buttering the pan
When shall she come with fungery
Knurled misshapen fruit of dark forest

Stood looking into iron pan
Sporting
Butter browning, too much waiting
Outside ferns sway be-spotted in sperm
Fungering

My butter is now truly burnt
Dark congealing bitterness
Looking to the path
Child returning slowly
Basketing mushrooms
Cradle me
Another lost child in the rain.

Argo

I fleecing argo
Talking in self
Squared one room
Signals me nothing
Only to return
On mammoth
Chattering starling poetry

Camera Obscura

I who sit with puppet
Wishing the sun off my face

The pelican dips and dips

On the left a sesame kiss
The dips of your lips shutting and opening
The puppets jaws, a spring to your waters

Voicer (sonnet maker)

Nip lipping my ear lobe, a pitch,
Taken quietly whilst I stand, ever wishing

Those pelican dips, bringing evening on,
A soiled tightness, acting a new performance
Of punch and judy, gaiety in sober
Red white and blue, sandy shores screeching
Child's delight

Marooned in the bar
The chinese girl dressed tartan-shirt
And hair-ribboned, raven fair,
Sporting jeans, stretched over the bar for more ice,

I the now mouth-less puppet,
Stroking her from afar

Moved,
Hear the grinding grit, under my boots

Glassed the puppets observation of the poet,
Shore-less when the summer season ends

Did I see a pelican shake beak or was it
Merely me walking into a winter's sea.

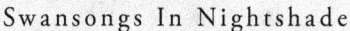

Rioja Lips

Sitting
Sizing one another up
Chess player word-moves
The stratagem, your face
Behind soft eyes
Love or indifference
I think its indifference
Offered cigarette, lit,
Ashtray forward pushed
Twin smoke, optical twins
Half lowered sang kindness
Will this look
Lead to a hot siesta, and the
Taste of rioja from your lips
Or corks in staling ashtrays.

Sabastina

My naked sabastian,
A human quiver for my arrows
How many times have I bored you
Milky body punctured in red
Stung with peppered lust
I turn you over my spit
When succulent I'll eat.

Kyrie

Have proclaimed blue cat
And a spotted seal
They beholden unto me
From not quite flat surfaces

Sun so hot
Burning ripples, stripes my face
Into real me, counterfeiting

Scooped up the last
Of the dying suns crown
Before the bats
Webbed into paradise

(Kyrie)

I and milton are one.

Little Sticks

Ysolt, lady with the white hands
Us meeting a while
In london's land of little sticks

Wagner echo, late saturday, afternoon

Where is now those patterned
Tracks of my fingers seen
To see, you must come up closer

Why have you shifted me to tristan's
Poison lance, did we not start from this point
Little sticks placed neatly
Consumpting my rage
Pyre lit by you.

Bus Stop

At the coming
Of the poet with soft eyes
She saw me at the bus stop
Not seeing her made no difference
To our conversion
Whilst glasses were clearly washed in rain
Softly finned in waters bright
Together we became otters in the night

She a young woman's
Shoulder blades, glistened
Mounting bus in light
Sweeping the curb, luscious in garbage

Fairly but lost her tail in the moonlight

I smothered over
In otter hounds bale delight.

Decay

Life wearing thin
Tired threadbare each hour
Sit waiting extremes
Partial slips of written paper
Would slip away quietly
But a forlorn wish

Petal browning
Crushed its scent
Life's book flower pressed
Leaving its staining tears
Mingled with words

The wind is hurricane
I sit
Killing myself slowly
With the fading blooms

Its late, very very late
Outside laughter in the night.

Lone Utterances

Butterflies settling
On the dead horses eyes
Craven cry, my olden flesh
No longer elastic
Backward ages, mind entered,
Reminiscent soft flesh,
Mine yours where went our sweet youth,
Broke with the tears
You mine know, breaking glass heart, aching,
Sweet one with the last but enough days
God willing were we to clasp hands,
Down to the web, gripping last nights call,
Yes the calling to a royal friend
Waste landing, scenting jasmine flow,
Like unto lone utterances of the jackal.

Hunger
A Day

Who pushed back
Coffee cup or love
Both a welcome at morning
Cigarettes chained through,
Sipping sherry, liven cure
Salted night left congealed,
Some where in tears
Chinked curtain of day
Speaking truth in morning
Proud magpie hushing lips
Of felon day
Creeping soft cares
Untangling yesterday's wolves
Of passion
All now completed in arch fire

For I Am The Vine Dresser

Small flying beetles drawn,
To the lamps white light,
Where their existence explodes
Leaving but their shells.
Empty shells like the written word,
The outer husks of its creation.
Meaningless, for they are not
What we meant to say, just a scrawl.
Where a touch, a kiss, a tear says everything.
But are we not trapped in egos gulag,
Prisoners to its pride,
When we tell it, it's wrong, arrogance laughs.
We would have the world share us,
For I am the vine dresser.
Caring all the clusters,
Whose moulding fruit, given as a poison for you.
We would have that life will leave something,
From its final wine-pressing,
Except the bloom mould
Smudged by Nemesis' fingers,
She plays our fruitless clusters,

John Wm. Giles

Crushing their juice into her cup,
Would she quaff the draft which is me.
For resting I would be,
The vine dressing, has worn my fingers raw,
With writing egos score,
Let the music play no more.

Drinking Song

With Socrates' hemlock,
The glass wearing my hand,
I lift my spirits with the drinking,
Abating the anger of the day.
Comfort and tears served well
With the imbibing poison,
Making me bold
In what my life will be.
Changes to be made, plans,
Yes so many plans,
Materializing in cigarette smoke,
Alcohol giving them body,
And the music so much music,
Coplands Appalachian Spring,
For I am the lord of the dance.
Mahlers Song of the Earth,
I the Chinese poet
Who sits and dreams
Of a land of silken flowers,
The dog of bronze
Howls into boundless infinity,

As if to mortify death of the poet.
I and my drunkenness are now one,
Firing the raging glory, till dawn.

Gaia Girl

The sorrow of swallows
My gaia girl has left
She will not be here
For the ripening pears
She beauty in green
And I left in blue tears,

John Wm. Giles

Broken Morning

Its a good day to be alive.
Quite morning, just me and the birds,
Cats crying to be let in
From their nights intrigues.
Their keepers slumber on
Until rising, switch their brains on
With breakfast T.V.,
Cats in, birds waiting
For soggy corn flakes and toast crusts,
As for me I'm alive (still)
Hoping that this will be that good day,
I've been forever waiting for,
Until I step outside
The first person I speak to
Then the days ruined,
The twisted tongue speaks
Counting on my madness, to always be
Unsold in their barren basement
Where their humanity never buys.
I ever waiting the plunge,
That dark falling

Where the weight of earthly stars
Cannot hold me up,
I sense their fickle indifference,
All the birds,
Have turned into diseased pigeons.

Anastasia 1918

Once upon a time
A small bird sat
A' singing between a wolfs ears
She perchance would clean his maw
Peck, peck, peck
One ruddy yawn and she was gone

One girl sliding down a wall
Torn and blood spattered
Business done
Room full smoke and stench
Of discharged shells, lingers
They turned and left
The one that sat outside smoking
Notice how it curled somewhat
Spiral up the bayonet
And pondered that there was
So much blood

The girl in lighted night repose
Silken soft in this place where

Swansongs In Nightshade

No one knows that little bird
Who cleans now her lip corners
And receives a much more
Sweeter kiss than you will
Ever know

Full Gifted Was His Sight

I and my friend
Went walking corridor streets,
Circumnavigating cul-de-sacs.
The placement of obstacles
Were a hindrance,
My friend pointed these out to me.
His castaway voice
Rang true, and like soft rain
Sang through me greatly,
Full gifted was his sight
He loved me, and I him,
Eternal circle of my life.
I the blind stumbling child
Held by strong hands.
Boulevard trees were no fear to us,
He guided both,
Even the empty voodoo populace
Whose bad mo-jo breed sickness, swerved,
For full gifted was his sight.

Then I fell through branches,

It was dark
I pulled back the curtains,
And let the moon in.

Suicide

My body and mind so broken
I am ready to leave now
Loop cord hanging from door

On my way to the far country
Where I might find a soft
And caring hand on mine
Or someone to hold both my hands
Or hold me in a gentle embrace
And say I am with you in your
Darkness and will lift you
Back into the light with my love.

Upon The Plains of Absalom

Whilst walking the plains of Absalom
With its pierced people and crucified horses,
I pondered the loss of myself.
Do those who say they love me, mean it,
Or are they slitting their tongues,
Wily serpents at my bosom.
Will I always fear that word, love,
Platitudes softened with honey
Rolling freely from kind hearts.
Holdings and the kiss upon the cheek,
Brutus loved Caesar deeply they say,
But weren't both crippled with its power,
What use this power, but a dust,
Soon scattered before the racing horses hooves.
This word love a control,
Used freely gnaws into many hearts
Only to be rent out, when bitterness enters,
Leaving the pierced upon the plains of Absalom.

John Wm. Giles

I'll wait upon this plain,
When day comes,
We'll see if their child's words
Do truly speak into my reticent heart
Or am I to be left crying,
Beneath the pierced and crucified,
For a thing that can never be had.

In the north, clouds are gathering
Brooding a vicious winter.
I, mammoths and the starlings waiting
Her loveless coming,
Is not our world tragic unto tears.
We will wait the sun-ships, full of spice,
Whose coming in spring,
Will bring new lovers
Upon the plains of Absalom.

"Sheila 1966"

She brought into the studio, hysteria
Promptly disposed in our black vase
Ask unto me, was all right
Lead eyes, said yes my love, smiled

I'll leave soon for a drink or two
After the ravens have settled
In splendour on her shoulders,

Leaves began to fall
When I closed the door
Her shoulders now full of birds.

A artist in the house
Linseed girl
Colouring my return
In her glorious rage
Ever falling her valhalla
My mad odin of the one eye
And brush
Slipped my boat upon her

Raging styx, her turps vagina
Then we laught into another day.

The years pass on
My linseed girl is somewhere now
In my lost need-hearts
So empty life.

Rain

Love,
Do we not leave the choicest morsel
Till last, relish in its savour,
That deep inner hunger, beckoning eagerly
To eat the surroundings, is this not love,
Gulp up you, leaving us with that soft morsel,
An oyster shell ripped, living swallowed,
Only one knows at morning-tide,
Spat out sickly lapped in the wave,
Gently at this time, did you not turn back,
Backed, came sunlight, you hidden in shade

Sleepily drinking into another afternoon,
Across fingers of pens, wrote for you
In sweet love of time and times of poetry,
Saw the deterioration of love in your eyes,
I a matter sinking in days, wield passes
Table full, I should read break my hand, lost in that
Love of you

John Wm. Giles

The door shut in a whimper,
I pressed glass, rain running down
You stepped all the puddles,
I muddled, room faced me full front,
Like the rain in your hair
Did I care

Rain
God, did I care
Rain
Fingers let go the harlot pen
Cried with the pain and rain,
You torrent in river-day.

Strange Birds

When riga moved away from the shore
Strange birds sang a terrible sorrow
Reaching greyness of waves
In which I shall find no rest
Tear-ducts accumulating sandy grains
Betrayed and lost again
I the ever failing child

But when riga moved away
Birds· strange flew
Crying travailed poet
Making riga a barren desert
O, for the taste of sand

Before leaving riga
The troll offered pure malt
, Stand fast that man
Pilot on-board
Sang the strange birds
I stood heaving
Brushing sand from my shoulders

John Wm. Giles

Turned to the vaughan brothers
Imploded in alchemy and god

Did I let my linnet fly?
Surrendered her voice for mine
Dead caging the small heart fading
A little voyager to a far country

Sand makes buildings strong
But where's my little linnets song
Thrown overboard flotsam on riga's shore
Whilst the poet seeks the way and true stone.

For Marion

Above my head
Head-board knocking
Another gentleman friend
Or death-watch beetle

Met her later in off-sales
She complained about loose floor-boards
I never had the trouble

Mandibles tapping
Walked her home.

Sunday, Puccini As Usual

Pressure cooker
Too come to terms with its-self
Sunday veg
Lieutenant whiskey, fly betrayed
Sherry half-pint with lemonade top
You're man downstairs turned up
To fix washing machine

White goods, like white gods dead
Beer for him, not to worry
Machine machine built to die

Geisha sundaying.

Soft Skinning Girls

Later tongued my bowl
Singapore fried noodle
Fired mouth
Birds flown
Then flocked

Taste-budding asia
Soft skinning the girls
Monsoon poet

A remorse
Of noodling words

I once again
Held in motherly girls arms
A soft release.

www.ingramcontent.com/pod-product-compliance
Lightning Source LLC
Chambersburg PA
CBHW050259120526
44590CB00016B/2417